Amazing
Insects

Duncan Searl

Upper Saddle River, New Jersey
www.globefearon.com

Executive Editor: Jean Liccione
Project Editor: Kim Choi
Supervising Editor: Lynn W. Kloss
Production Editor: Amy Benefiel
Senior Designer: Janice Noto-Helmers
Electronic Page Production: Jeffrey Engel
Editorial Assistant: Jennifer Watts

Globe
Fearon

1-800-321-3106
www.globefearon.com

Contents

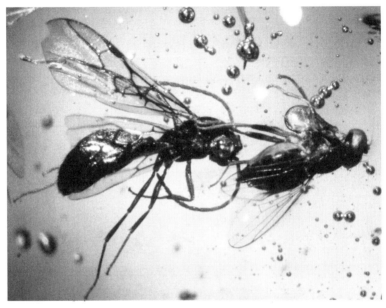

Insects have lived on Earth for 350 million years. This photograph shows two flies that lived some 40 million years ago.

Chapter One
The World of Insects

About 80 percent of all the animals on Earth are insects. Scientists have already named more than a million **species**, or different kinds. Each year, they find thousands more. At least 100,000 species live in the United States.

What is the total number of insects in the world? No one knows. Insects multiply too fast to count them all. Each female cabbage aphid, for example, has 40 offspring. Each of those baby aphids will have offspring within two weeks. By the end of the fall, a single aphid could have trillions of descendants!

When insects swarm in large groups, we get an idea of their great numbers. One swarm of locusts, for example, was 300 miles long and 100 miles wide. There were about 125 billion locusts in that swarm!

Insects can adapt to many kinds of places. They can even live where no other animals can survive. Insects live in the frozen Arctic. They live on the highest mountains in South America. Blind insects live in underground caves. Others live in hot springs where the temperature is 120°F.

Insects have lived on Earth for 350 million years. Scientists have found fossils of insects in rocks. Some of these rocks are 300 million years old. These fossils show what insects were like long ago. Ancient insects were much like today's insects. They had the same body parts. However, some were much larger than today's insects. Dragonflies, for example, once had a wingspan of 30 inches. That is four times bigger than today's dragonflies.

Today, most insects are small. Their size helps them survive. Insects can live on tiny specks of food. A drop of dew is plenty of water for a thirsty insect. Many small insects spend their whole lives inside a single seed or leaf. There, they find food and safety.

Insects vary in size and shape. The dwarf blue butterfly of South America is less than $\frac{1}{2}$ inch wide. Some beetles are much smaller than the head of a pin. One wasp is less than $\frac{1}{100}$ of an inch long.

Giant walking stick

The giant walking stick is one of the largest insects. It is up to 13 inches long. The Atlas moth of Asia is another large insect. It measures 12 inches across. The world's largest fly is the robber fly of South America. It is $2\frac{1}{2}$ inches long. The heaviest insect of all is the Goliath beetle of Africa. It weighs about 3 ounces.

6

Goliath beetle of Africa

This book should help you see insects in a new way. You will learn why insects are important to people. You will also understand why insects are so common. The book describes the body features and habits that most insects have in common. At the same time, it shows some of the endless differences among insects. These differences make insects some of the most fascinating animals on Earth.

Chapter Two
What Is an Insect?

Unlike other animals, insects do not have backbones. They do not have bones at all. Instead, they have a tough covering on the outside of their bodies. This covering is called the **exoskeleton**. The Greek prefix *exo-* means "outside." The exoskeleton holds water in the insect's body. It keeps the body from drying up.

All insects have six legs. This fact will help you identify insects. Spiders and scorpions, for example, have eight legs. So they are not insects. Worms have no legs. So they are not insects either. Snails have just one big foot. So they cannot be insects. Centipedes have up to 350 legs. They are not insects either.

Most insects also have a unique body shape. The word *insect* comes from a Latin word that means "cut into." The body of an insect looks "cut into" at the middle. You can see this shape in ants and wasps.

The Three Parts of an Insect's Body

All insects have the same three body parts: the head, the thorax, and the abdomen. At the front of every insect is the head. The head's job is to find and eat food. Most adult insects have two bulging eyes on their head. These are called **compound eyes** because they are made up of many tiny **lenses**. Compound eyes can see motion and color. Most insects also have three **simple eyes** with single lenses. These eyes sense light. They tell the insect if it is day or night.

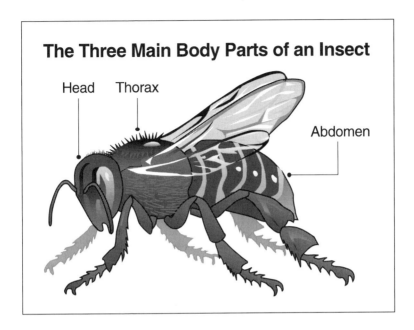

The Three Main Body Parts of an Insect

Head   Thorax

Abdomen

Mouths and antennae are also on the insect's head. Mouths come in all shapes and sizes, depending on what the insect eats. The mouth of a grasshopper can bite and chew leaves. The mouth of a mosquito can cut skin and suck blood. A butterfly usually sucks nectar from flowers. So its mouth is a long tube.

Antennae help insects find food by touch and smell. Most insects have two antennae. The antennae of some insects are so small that you cannot see them. Other insects have antennae that are longer than their bodies. Antennae can look like feathers, threads, strings of beads, or clubs.

Behind the head is the **thorax**. It is the second part of an insect's body. The thorax is the insect's center of movement. It holds the legs and the wings.

The **abdomen** is the third and largest part of an insect's body. It holds the heart, stomach, and sex organs. An insect also breathes through its abdomen. It takes in air through tiny holes called **spiracles**. Tubes then carry the air through the body.

Insect Wings

An insect's wings have thin skin stretched over its veins. Most insects have two pairs of wings that flap together. A dragonfly, however, uses each pair of wings separately. That allows it to **hover**, or fly in place.

Beetles and cockroaches have front wings that are stiff. These cover the delicate back wings, which the insects use to fly. Flies use only their front wings. Their back wings are just knobs. These knobs help them fly at a steady height. The wings of moths and butterflies have scales. These scales give the wings their amazing colors and patterns.

A dragonfly has two pairs of wings. It uses each pair separately.

A ladybug (a type of beetle) has stiff front wings that cover the delicate back wings.

Insect Legs

Each insect has legs and feet that suit the way it moves. Water beetles have wide legs that work like paddles. A flea's foot has long claws for hanging onto an animal's body. Grasshoppers can jump well because their legs are long and flexible. A housefly's foot has suction pads on it. The pads let the fly climb up glass or crawl across a ceiling upside-down.

The Insect Family Tree

There are about a million species in the class of animals called *Insecta*. That word means "insects." Scientists divide the class into smaller groups called **orders**. The largest order of insects—beetles—has 300,000 species. Another order—butterflies and moths—has 100,000 species. The order of wasps, bees, and ants has 115,000 species.

The Insect Family Tree on page 12 shows the most important insect orders. The family tree gives the scientific name of each order. The closer two orders are on the tree, the more alike they are.

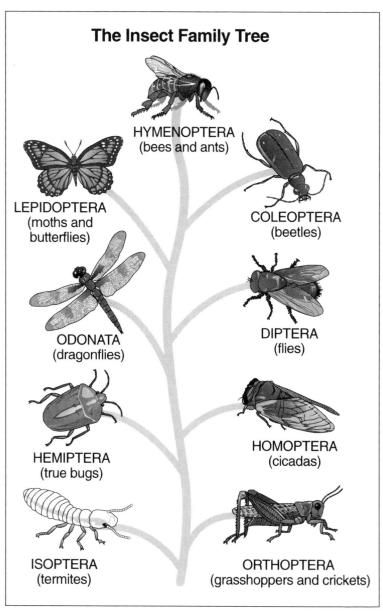

The Insect Family Tree

HYMENOPTERA
(bees and ants)

LEPIDOPTERA
(moths and
butterflies)

COLEOPTERA
(beetles)

ODONATA
(dragonflies)

DIPTERA
(flies)

HEMIPTERA
(true bugs)

HOMOPTERA
(cicadas)

ISOPTERA
(termites)

ORTHOPTERA
(grasshoppers and crickets)

The beetles (Coleoptera), flies (Diptera), butterflies and moths (Lepidoptera), and wasps, bees, and ants (Hymenoptera) are the largest orders of insects.

Chapter Three
How Insects Grow

Almost all insects hatch from eggs. Some insect eggs are as large as a capital *O*. Others are so tiny that you cannot see them without a microscope.

Some insects lay just one egg. Others lay thousands of eggs at a time. Some insects just drop their eggs on the ground. Others bury their eggs or drop them into water. Many insects stick their eggs to leaves or bushes. Others lay them inside dead animals. One tiny wasp lays her eggs inside the eggs of a moth. Giant female water bugs lay their eggs on the backs of male water bugs.

Insects lay their eggs near a good food supply. Once the eggs hatch, the young insects are on their own. If there is plenty of food nearby, the young insects are more likely to survive.

Metamorphosis

After they hatch, insects go through several changes before becoming adults. This series of changes is called **metamorphosis**.

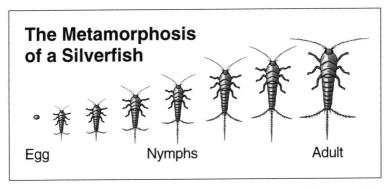

The Metamorphosis of a Silverfish

Egg   Nymphs   Adult

When a silverfish hatches, it already looks like a tiny adult silverfish.

When some insects hatch, they already look like tiny adults. They simply grow larger. They shed their exoskeleton several times and each time grow a new one. Other baby insects look almost like adults. All they are missing is their wings. They get bigger and shed their exoskeletons several times before they finally grow wings.

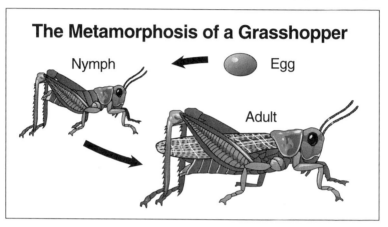

The Metamorphosis of a Grasshopper

Nymph ← Egg

Adult

A grasshopper, when it hatches, looks almost like an adult grasshopper, except it has no wings.

The most advanced insects develop in four stages: egg, larva, pupa, and adult. This is called **complete metamorphosis**. Flies, moths, butterflies, bees, and beetles develop this way.

In complete metamorphosis, a **larva** hatches from an egg. This larva looks completely different from an adult. The larva of a butterfly is a caterpillar. The larva of a fly is a maggot.

Insect larvae grow quickly. Then they take a rest. This rest period is called the **pupa** stage. Many pupae have special coverings. Moths, for example, spin cocoons to protect themselves during the pupa stage. Bees and wasps make cocoons of wax.

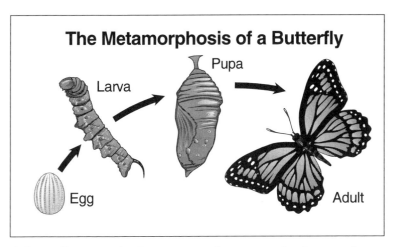

The Metamorphosis of a Butterfly

Larva

Pupa

Egg

Adult

A butterfly grows in four stages of metamorphosis: egg, larva, pupa, and adult.

From the outside, a pupa looks quiet. Inside, though, many changes are taking place. All of its old body parts dissolve and disappear. New body parts form. The whole body changes into its adult form.

When the pupa's skin splits open, the adult insect crawls out. The exoskeleton is soft at first, but it soon hardens. The new adult has a full set of wings. These wings must expand and dry before the insect can fly. After a few minutes, the adult flies away, to search for food.

Most adult insects do not live very long. Some live just a few days or a few weeks. Their purpose is to find mates and produce eggs. Then the whole cycle starts all over again.

Chapter Four
An Inside Look at Insects

What goes on inside the tiny body of an insect? The body organs of insects are very different from those of mammals. Still, their organs do the same jobs. These include breathing, circulating blood, digesting food, and getting messages from the outside world.

Insect Breathing

Insects do not have noses or lungs for breathing. Instead, they have a system of air tubes, called **tracheae**, inside their bodies.

Most insects have a row of openings on their abdomens to let in air. These openings are called spiracles. Small valves open and close the spiracles. Insects can pump their abdomens up and down to push more air into their spiracles.

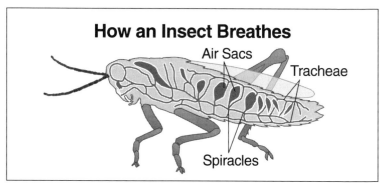

How an Insect Breathes

Air Sacs

Tracheae

Spiracles

Air enters through the spiracles and moves through the tracheae.

Insect Blood

An animal's **circulatory system** moves blood through the body. The blood carries food to all the parts of the body. It also carries waste out of the body.

Mammals have many tubes called **blood vessels**. Their blood always stays inside the blood vessels. An insect, however, has only one blood vessel. Its blood flows out of this blood vessel. Then the blood moves freely through the insect's body.

An insect's blood vessel is at the top of its body. Part of this blood vessel is the heart. The heart pumps blood to the head. Then the blood flows out of the blood vessel. It washes over all the cells of the body. In the lower abdomen, the blood drains back into the blood vessel. Then the heart pumps it back to the head.

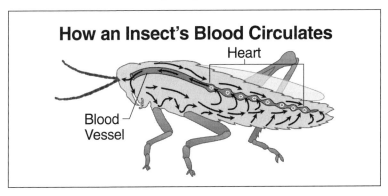

How an Insect's Blood Circulates

Heart

Blood Vessel

The rear part of the insect's blood vessel is the heart. Blood is pumped toward the head. From there, it moves through the body.

Insect blood can be yellow, green, brown, white, or red. Often, it has no color at all. Some insect blood is poisonous to other animals. The blood of many beetles, for example, causes human skin to blister.

Insect Digestion

An animal must break down, or **digest**, its food before its body can use it. An insect's **digestive system** is a long tube that begins in the mouth, where saliva starts to break down the food.

Next, food passes down to the **crop**. The crop stores the food and breaks it down further. When the food is completely digested, the blood carries it through the body. At the end of the digestion tube, water is removed from the food wastes. Then the wastes pass out of the insect's body.

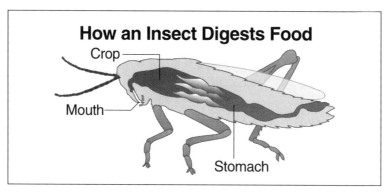

How an Insect Digests Food

Crop

Mouth

Stomach

The digestive tract of most insects is one long tube.

Insect Nerves

An insect's **nervous system** includes a brain, two **nerve cords**, and nerve centers called **ganglia**. The brain controls the insect's eyes and antennae. Two nerve cords run the length of an insect's body. Along these cords are the ganglia. The ganglia control actions such as walking, flying, and breathing.

Insect Senses

Like most animals, insects have five main senses. These are sight, hearing, smell, touch, and taste. Different insects use different senses to help them find food. Bees have powerful eyes. As they search for flowers, they can see parts of sunlight that people cannot see. Horseflies, too, have good eyesight. They fly by day and need to find animals to bite. Moths, on the other hand, fly at night and hardly use their eyes at all. They find food by using their sense of smell.

For many insects, the world is a pattern of smells and tastes. Ants, for example, lay down a trail of smells as they search for food. Following the trail, other ants will also find the food. As they work, ants constantly touch one another. In this way, they pass on their nest smell to each other.

Their sense of smell helps insects survive in other ways, too. When danger is near, many insects make alarm chemicals. These chemicals have a special smell. The smell tells other insects to be on guard. When it is time to gather together, or swarm, insects spread the word with a different chemical smell.

Female moths release a special smell to attract males from far away. Females release chemicals after laying their eggs, too. The smell of the chemicals sends a message to other insects. The message of the smell is, "My eggs are here. Go somewhere else to lay yours."

Insects use their antennae to smell and touch things. Different kinds of insects have different kinds of antennae. Often, males and females of the same species have very different antennae.

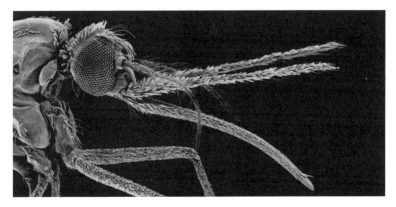

Antennae of a female mosquito

A butterfly's antennae are covered with fine hairs. These hairs help the insect feel air currents as it flies. A female mosquito's long, feathery antennae sense heat from warm-blooded bodies. These antennae help her find food in the dark. Many beetles have large, fan-shaped antennae. The fans are usually closed. From time to time, the beetle opens them to smell the direction of its next meal.

The world of insects includes sounds that humans never hear. Different kinds of insects use different parts of their bodies to feel sound vibrations. Ants pick up vibrations through their feet. The vibrations tell them when an enemy is near.

Grasshoppers and locusts have ears on their abdomens. These ears receive messages sent by other grasshoppers or locusts. A cockroach uses long bristles on its body to "hear" anything moving toward it. Other insects pick up sound vibrations with their long, delicate wings.

No one knows for sure exactly what insects see, hear, smell, taste, and feel. Scientists are just beginning to explore how insect senses work. As scientists study insect senses, they are sure to learn more amazing facts about these fascinating creatures.

Chapter Five
Insect Defenses

Many insect eggs never hatch. Many baby insects never become adults. Nature is hard on insects. Heat, frost, drought, floods, and disease destroy many eggs and larvae.

Insects also have many animal enemies. Birds poke through dirt and leaves looking for insects. They also grab them in the air. Bears and skunks paw through rotting logs to eat insects. In the water, hungry fish hunt for insects. Large insects even gobble up smaller insects. The blue-green searcher beetle runs up and down twigs, eating caterpillars as fast as it can. Lacewing larvae even eat their own brothers and sisters. Against these odds, how do insects survive? How do they defend themselves?

Strength in Numbers

According to an old saying, "There is strength in numbers." Insects seem to have learned this lesson. A female insect, for example, may lay 20,000 eggs in one mating season. Even if 99.9 percent of them never hatch, 20 eggs might reach adulthood. That is more than enough for the species to survive and grow.

Insects also mature quickly. It does not take long for a young female insect to become an adult and lay eggs. Twenty generations of fruit flies, for example, are born in a single year.

Flight, Not Fight

Many insects escape their enemies by flying or running away. A dragonfly can fly 50 feet per second to escape a bird. Even scientists have a hard time catching dragonflies!

21

Houseflies are among the slowest-flying insects. They usually fly about 5 miles per hour. However, they can go much faster if necessary.

Butterflies and bees cruise along at 13 miles per hour. Horseflies average 25 miles per hour. However, they, too, can go much faster to escape danger.

When it comes to running away, cockroaches deserve a medal. A cockroach can zigzag 25 times in a single second! Signals from its antennae tell the cockroach when to change direction.

Leaping away is another insect skill. A grasshopper can leap 20 times its body length. If you could do this, you could cross the length of a football field in three jumps. You could leap over a five-story building in a single bound! Fleas and crickets are also amazing jumpers.

Dropping down and playing dead is another insect defense. Many caterpillars will drop from a bush as soon as you touch them. On the ground below, they lie still. They often escape because they are hard to see in the grass. The giant water bug also plays dead when danger is near. It can lie still for hours.

Grasshoppers are the jumping champions of the insect world.

The click beetle varies this trick a little. When a bird attacks it, the beetle makes a loud clicking noise. The startled bird often drops the beetle to the ground. There, the beetle plays dead and is usually left alone.

Moths drop and hide, too. Bats try to catch them in the air. To find the moths, bats give off high squeaks and listen for the echo. Many moths can hear these bat squeaks. When they do, they drop to the ground, where the bats cannot find them.

Camouflage

Camouflage means "blending in with the surroundings." Many insects blend in so well with their surroundings that their enemies never spot them. Green caterpillars are the same color as the leaves they eat. Walking sticks look just like twigs. Thorn bugs look just like thorns. Gray moths are the same color as the bark of their favorite trees. Some small bugs are almost transparent, or see-through. The color of the leaf under them is all an enemy sees.

This thorn bug blends in with its surroundings.

Butterflies use camouflage in special ways. The larvae of swallowtail butterflies look just like bird droppings, so birds leave them alone. Many adult butterflies land facing the sun. Then they fold their wings straight up above their backs. They cast no shadows, and their enemies are not likely to see them.

The Kallima butterfly has the best trick of all. As it flies through the air, its bright wings look tasty to a hungry bird. When the Kallima senses danger, however, it lands. Then it holds its wings together so that only the undersides show. The undersides are pale brown. They look like an old leaf.

Built-in Weapons

Many insects have built-in ways to defend themselves. Bees and wasps have stingers. Birds know how painful those stings are. So they avoid the insects.

The bombardier beetle got its name by setting off "bombs." When it is attacked, two chemicals from its body flow into a small sac in its abdomen. There, the chemicals mix and explode. A puff of black smoke bursts out the back end of the beetle. This smoke blocks the enemy's view while the beetle escapes.

Insects have many other kinds of defenses. Stinkbugs and lacewings produce a terrible smell if they are disturbed. Wood ants squirt acid at their enemies. Monarch butterflies taste so bad that birds leave them alone.

The puss-moth caterpillar is the king of defense. First of all, it has hairs that sting an attacker. It can also produce a false pair of horns to scare an attacker away. Finally, it can squirt acid at its enemies.

Insect Mimics

A **mimic** pretends to be something other than what it is. Some insects look like more dangerous insects. Bee flies, for examples, are fat flies that look like bees. They buzz and have thick hair, but they do not have stingers. Birds do not know that, though. So birds avoid bee flies just as they avoid bees. The harmless hoverfly looks like a hornet. The African ground beetle looks like a poisonous ant.

Some moths and bugs can even look like owls and cats. These big insects have patterns on their back wings. The patterns look like the eyes of a cat or an owl. Most of the time, the insect keeps these "eyes" hidden. When an enemy is near, however, the insect flashes its eye pattern. The attacker thinks that a real cat or owl is nearby. So it goes away.

On their back wings, some moths have a pattern that looks like the eyes of an owl.

The No-Defense Defense

Cicadas seem to have no defenses. They cannot run, fly, or jump away. They cannot sting or bite. They do not play dead. They have no camouflage, and birds and animals think they taste fine.

How do cicadas survive? Every 12 or 17 years, cicadas hatch by the millions. They come up from underground for their brief adult lives. Other animals eat their fill of cicadas, but it really does not matter. There just are not enough enemies to eat all of them. Many cicadas survive to lay their eggs, and the species lives on.

Chapter Six
The Amazing Ants

There are about 8,000 different kinds of ants. All ants look alike, except in size and color. They all have a narrow "waist" between their thorax and their abdomen. With their strong jaws, they can deliver a painful bite. Some ants sting, and other ants squirt acid at their enemies.

Ants are social insects. They live together in a colony. The colony centers on its queen. There may be as many as 100,000 ants in a colony, but there is only one queen. She spends all her time laying eggs.

Most ants in a colony are workers. These ants never stop working. They build the nest. They keep it clean. They hunt for food. They take care of the queen and the young ants. They feed them and protect them.

In many ways, ant colonies are like human cities. Busy ant "cities" can last for hundreds of years. Compared to other insects, ants live a long time. Some workers may live up to 7 years. Some queens continue laying eggs for up to 15 years.

To find their way, ants follow trails of smell left by other ants in the colony.

Near an ant nest, streams of ants can be seen walking along a trail. As the trail gets farther from the nest, the ants spread out to look for food. When the ants return home on the trail, they carry food in their jaws. To find their way, ants follow trails of smell left by other ants. Some ants can also use the sun as a compass.

Different species of ants eat different kinds of food. Some ants even grow their own food. Among the most amazing eaters are Amazon ants, army ants, leaf-cutter ants, and honey ants.

Amazon Ants

Amazon ants are fierce fighters. They fight their way into the nests of other ants. The other ants fight back, but the Amazon ants always win. After a successful attack, the Amazons steal the young ants of their enemy and carry them home.

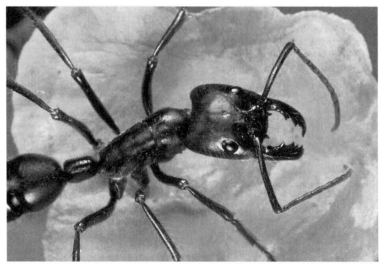

Amazon ants are fierce fighters that attack other ants' nests.

When the captured ants grow up, they become the Amazons' "enslaved ants." They dig and build nests for their masters. They go out and find food for the Amazons. They even feed their masters. In fact, the Amazons have forgotten how to feed themselves. Even if food is piled all around them, they will starve if their helpers are not there to feed them.

Army ants make a bridge for other army ants to cross a river.

Army Ants

Most ants live in one place all their lives. The army ants of Africa, however, are always on the move. From time to time, millions of these ants march together across the countryside. Along the way, they eat every insect, bird, or other small animal they can find. They simply swarm all over the helpless animal and start eating. Army ants will even eat humans or elephants that cannot run away.

Strong sunshine can kill army ants. So they usually march at night or on cloudy days. Rivers also slow them down because they cannot swim well. The water only slows them down for a while, however. Soon, they have built their own ant bridge across the river.

Here is how these amazing ants build a bridge: With their strong jaws, a few ants take hold of a root or bush on the riverbank. Other ants take hold of these ants. Soon there is a "rope" of ants. The water carries this "rope" to the other side of the river. The rest of the ants then march across this bridge. On the opposite shore, they continue their search for food.

After a few weeks of searching for food, the army ants settle down. They form a huge ball. The ball is like a normal ant nest, except that the walls are made of ants! Inside are tunnels and walls formed from the ants' bodies. The queen lives near the middle. She begins to lay eggs. When the eggs hatch, the army ants take good care of the young. Once these babies grow up, the ants get ready for another move.

Ant Farmers

Leaf-cutters are the farmers of the ant world. These little ants cut down small bits of leaves. Then they carry the leaves into their underground nests. They chew the leaves and spread them out in tiny "fields." Then they plant a **fungus** on the leaves. A fungus is a simple plant in the same family as molds and mushrooms. Before long, tiny white swellings appear on the fungus. The ants bite these off for food.

Other ants raise their own "cows." These "cows" are actually tiny insects called aphids, or "ant cows." Aphids eat a sweet liquid called **honeydew**, which they suck from plants. Ants like this honeydew, too. So they keep aphids in their nests to supply honeydew.

Leaf-cutter ants carry small bits of leaves into their nests.

To "milk" an aphid, an ant gently taps and strokes the aphid with its antennae. Out comes a drop of honeydew. In one day, an aphid can supply 48 drops of honeydew for the ants.

Ants also keep other insects as pets. Tiny beetles are popular pets. Some scientists believe that the beetles give off a smell that the ants enjoy. Scientists have watched ants pet their beetles or carry them on their backs.

Honey Ants

Honey ants have a special way of storing extra food. Like all ants, the honey ants have two stomachs. One is the ant's own stomach. The other is used to carry food to other ants in the colony. Worker ants give the food from this second stomach to the queen and to young ants.

Honey ants also store extra honeydew in their second stomachs. When they have food left over, they feed it to young workers. When times are good, some of these worker ants get so fat that they cannot move. They hang from the ceiling of the nest until the colony needs their food. When the dry season comes, there is very little food outside. Then the whole colony feeds on the food inside these "living refrigerators."

Chapter Seven
The Busy Bees

Long ago, people learned to like honeybees. A 9,000-year-old cave painting in Spain shows a man taking honey from a wild honeybee nest. The ancient Egyptians began keeping their own bees more than 2,500 years ago. Today, bees make honey and beeswax worth millions of dollars. They also carry pollen from flower to flower. This action is called **pollination**. The pollination process helps countless flowers, fruits, vegetables, and field crops to bear fruit.

A beekeeper checks her beehives.

Three Kinds of Bees in a Hive

Worker

Drone

Queen

There are three kinds of bees in a hive: workers, drones, and a queen. As many as 60,000 bees may live in one hive.

The Members of the Hive

A beehive is like a city of wax. It is made from thousands of small six-sided cells. In some of the cells, the bees store food. In other cells, the queen lays eggs. The larvae hatch from the eggs and then grow into pupae without ever leaving the cells.

As many as 60,000 bees may live in one hive, or colony. Each hive has three kinds of bees: workers, drones, and a queen.

Worker bees fly from flower to flower to gather **nectar**, which is a sweet liquid found in flowers. Bees use the nectar to make honey. Most of the bees in a colony are workers. They do all the chores in the hive. The workers are female, but they do not lay eggs.

The drones are the male bees. There are only a few drones in each colony. Their only job is to mate with the queen.

There is one queen in each colony. Her only duty is to lay eggs. A queen may live 4 or 5 years and may lay as many as half a million eggs. The queen is larger than the worker bees, but she is not as heavy as the drones.

The workers feed the larvae until they turn into pupae.

Feeding the Young

When the bee eggs hatch into larvae, the workers take care of them. First, they feed the larvae royal jelly, a liquid made by the workers. Later, they feed the larvae honey and pollen. After a week, the larvae become pupae. When they hatch, they go to work for the colony.

A few of the larvae receive special care. They live in larger cells and eat only royal jelly. These larvae grow larger than the others do. After turning into pupae, they begin to hatch. The first pupa to hatch stings the others to death. She becomes the new queen bee for the hive.

A beehive can have only one queen. When the new queen is born, the old queen flies away. Usually, the old queen takes several thousand workers with her. At first, this new swarm gathers on a tree branch. Scouts from the swarm search for a new home. When they find one, the swarm moves in and the workers build a new hive.

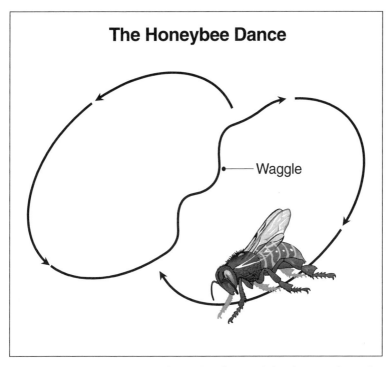

The Honeybee Dance

Waggle

A honeybee adds the waggle to its figure-eight dance when the food source is far away. The faster the waggle, the farther the distance to the food source.

The Dance of the Bees

When a honeybee finds flowers, it gathers nectar and stores the food in a pouch in its body. Then it returns to the hive. There, it dances to tell the other bees where the flowers are.

If the flowers are nearby, the worker does a quick series of figure-eight loops. This "round" dance excites the other workers. They touch their antennae to the returning worker to get the smell of the flowers. That way, they will be able to find the flowers easily. If the bee has found many flowers, it dances very fast. If it has found just a few flowers, it dances slowly.

If the flowers are far away, the worker does a "tail waggling" dance. In this dance, the bee moves its abdomen from side to side as it dances. Again, it makes a series of figure-eight loops. The farther the food is from the hive, the smaller the loops and the faster the waggling.

Bees also use the position of the sun to tell where the food supply is. If the food is in the direction of the sun, the dancer moves toward the top of the hive. If the food is in the direction opposite the sun, the dancer moves to the bottom of the hive. As the position of the sun changes, the angle of the bee's dance also changes.

Honeybees store honey in the six-sided cells of their hive.

Honey Makers

There are thousands of kinds of bees. However, only a few of them store honey. Most bees simply live day-by-day, eating nectar where they find it.

To make honey, worker bees use their long tongues to suck up drops of nectar from flowers. The bees have special "honey" stomachs to store the nectar. Chemicals in bees' stomachs mix with the nectar as they fly home.

When the workers get home, they place their nectar into empty cells of the hive. The water in the nectar soon **evaporates**. It turns into a gas called water vapor and disappears into the air. As the water evaporates, the chemicals from the worker's stomach change the nectar into honey.

Chapter Eight
Butterflies and Moths

Butterflies are among the most beautiful of all insects. Their bright colors and graceful flying have inspired artists and poets around the world.

Butterflies and moths belong to a group of insects called *Lepidoptera.* That word means "scaly-winged." Butterflies and moths are covered with tiny scales. The scales overlap like tiles on a roof. These scales create beautiful colors when light shines on them.

There are more than 180,000 kinds of butterflies. The largest butterflies have wingspans of 10 inches or more. The smallest are no bigger than a child's fingernail. Rainforests have the most kinds of butterflies. However, these beautiful insects also live in mountains, deserts, woods, and fields.

What is the difference between a moth and a butterfly? Moths tend to have fatter bodies and duller colors than butterflies. Unlike butterflies, moths do not have knobs on the ends of their antennae. Moths fly at dusk. Butterflies, on the other hand, show off their colors in bright sunshine.

A moth rests with its wings spread out flat.

A butterfly rests with its wings pressed together overhead.

Finally, the two insects fold their wings differently. A moth rests with its wings spread out flat. A resting butterfly presses its wings together overhead.

A Butterfly's Life Story

Most butterflies grow up in the same way. Here is the life story of the black swallowtail butterfly.

The female swallowtail usually lays her eggs on carrot leaves. Like most butterflies, swallowtails eat only one type of plant. They will starve to death if they cannot get this food. Luckily, the female knows which plant her young will eat.

Swallowtail eggs look like drops of dew. Their appearance fools birds and other enemies into leaving the eggs alone. Long ago, people even thought that dewdrops grew into butterflies!

After a few days, the eggs turn black. Little, spiny caterpillars crawl out. At first, they eat the shells of their eggs. Then they may gobble up carrot leaves.

When a caterpillar is about 2 inches long, it spins some silk. It uses the silk to attach its tail to a branch. Next, it spins more silk and fastens its neck to the branch.

As the caterpillar sways in the breeze, an amazing change occurs. The skin along its back splits open. Out comes the soft green pupa. The pupa wriggles back and forth until all the caterpillar skin has fallen away.

The pupa of a butterfly is called a **chrysalis**. The word comes from the Greek word for *gold*. A chrysalis often has a bright golden color. Slowly, the chrysalis dries and hardens.

Inside the chrysalis, the old body parts of the caterpillar change into a butterfly. That takes several weeks. One day, the upper end of the chrysalis breaks open. The wet and crumpled butterfly struggles out. The new adult swallowtail waits for its wings to dry and harden. Then it soars off, searching for food.

A new butterfly emerges from its chrysalis.

Monarch butterflies gather on a tree before migrating to a warmer place.

The Flight of the Monarch

Most moths and butterflies die in the frosty nights of autumn. In spring, a new generation of moths or butterflies will hatch, or come out of their cocoons. Some moths and butterflies do survive the winter, though. They hide under tree bark or in other safe places. The spring weather brings them out to lay eggs.

Some butterflies escape the cold weather by **migrating**, or traveling to a warmer place. The orange-and-black monarch butterfly travels the farthest. Dense clouds of monarchs leave Canada and the northern

United States each fall. Usually, they gather on a tree or bush before beginning the long flight south. Most of them head for California, Florida, or Mexico. They often must fly 2,000 miles or more. Strangely enough, monarchs usually fly to the same forests each year.

Monarch butterflies spend the winter resting. Swarms of them cover whole forests. They have to save energy to make the long flight back north in the spring. Scientists place tiny tags on the wings of monarchs. Then they wait to see where the tagged butterflies end up.

As they fly north, the monarchs fade in color. They lose scales from their wings. Many do not make it all the way north. The females, however, lay eggs along the way. After the young ones mature, they continue the trip north.

Many monarchs survive because they taste bad to birds. Birds soon learn to recognize monarchs and leave them alone. Another orange-and-black butterfly, the viceroy, also benefits. The viceroy tastes fine to birds. However, since it looks so much like the monarch, birds usually leave it alone, too!

Monarch butterfly   **Viceroy butterfly**

The Silk Spinners

The silkworm is not a worm at all. It is a caterpillar. If it is left alone, it turns into a moth.

People do not leave silkworms alone, though. Instead, they put the insects to work. Farmers in Asia raise billions of them. The farmers also grow mulberry trees because silkworms eat mulberry leaves.

A few weeks after it hatches, a silkworm enters its pupa stage. A very thin thread comes out of its mouth. The silkworm moves its head from side to side, wrapping the thread around its body. Three days later, the silkworm is inside a cocoon of silk thread.

Farmers then put the cocoons into a hot oven or into boiling water. That kills the insect inside. Then farmers send the cocoons to a silk factory.

At the factory, machines unwind the cocoons. Other machines then spin the thin threads together. Later, these threads are woven into silk cloth. It takes about 20,000 cocoons to make a pound of silk cloth.

Silkworm farmers let some of the silkworms live. These insects become moths. The adult moths live just a few days. Before it dies, the female moth lays hundreds of eggs. Soon, new silkworms are busily spinning silk.

A worker harvests silkworm cocoons in the Zhejiang province of China.

Three Amazing Moths

Among the most beautiful moths in the world are the Io, the Luna, and the Polyphemus. All three have velvety wings and measure more than 3 inches across.

The Io moth has big round eyespots and brilliant red-and-yellow wings. The Luna moth is pale green, with two long tails that flow like ribbons. The Polyphemus moth is blue, yellow, pearl, and brown.

Surprisingly, not one of these amazing moths ever eats. They come out of their cocoons at night and fly around in the dark. They mate and lay their eggs. Then, after just a few days of life, they die.

Io moth

Luna moth

Polyphemus moth

The Moth and the Flame

Many insects fly toward bright lights. Moths, in particular, have a deadly attraction to lights. Often, a moth will fly closer and closer to a candle until it burns itself.

Why does this happen? Bright lights interfere with the moth's ability to find its way in the dark. Usually, moths fly in straight lines. They use a distant light, such as the moon, as a compass. The moon helps them to fly in the right direction. When a moth uses a candle as its compass, the system does not work. The moth circles around the flame, again and again, trying to find its way. It may even fly right into the flame.

Chapter Nine
Meet the Beetles

Beetles are the most successful species on our planet. One in every four species on Earth is a beetle. There are at least 250,000 different kinds.

Beetles eat all kinds of plants and animals—dead or alive. Many beetles are pests. They attack crops and stored food. On the other hand, beetles also eat dead plants and animals. By doing this, they help clean up the planet and enrich the soil. Beetles are also an important part of the food chain. Birds, reptiles, and small mammals depend on them for food.

A beetle's eggs hatch into larvae called **grubs**. Some grubs feed for several years before becoming adults. Adult beetles come in all sizes. The tiny fungus beetle, for example, is much smaller than the period at the end of this sentence. The giant Goliath beetle, the world's heaviest insect, grows up to 6 inches long.

Beetles are an important part of Earth's food chain.

Beetles have the heaviest exoskeletons of all insects. These exoskeletons are like armor. As beetles crawl along, they look like little army tanks. For other insects, beetles are just as hard to attack as tanks.

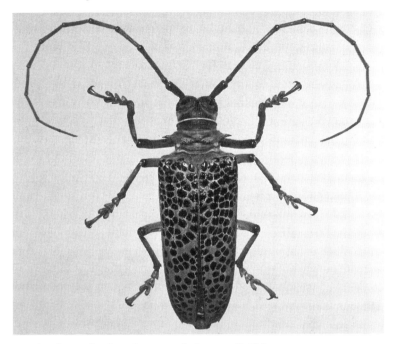

Beetles have the heaviest exoskeleton of all insects.

Beetles also have hard, heavy front wings that join in the middle of their backs. These front wings cover and protect the delicate back wings. Beetles use their back wings for flying.

Among the most amazing beetles are the firefly, the dung beetle, the ladybug, and the long-horned beetle.

Flying Light

Fireflies are also called glowworms or lightning bugs. However, they are neither flies nor worms. They are beetles. Dozens of different beetles have the ability to light up. Their bodies make a chemical that gives off light when it mixes with oxygen.

On summer nights, a male firefly takes to the air, flashing his light. Each species of flying beetle has its own light code. Some light up brighter or longer than others. Some flash their lights more often than others.

A female firefly usually rests on a plant. She watches the sky for the flash of her species. When she sees it, she signals back in the same code. After sending a few signals, the two beetles find each other and mate.

Fireflies die just a few days after mating. Their eggs hatch as larvae that look like worms. After several months, each larva buries itself underground. When it becomes an adult, the firefly chews its way to the surface and searches for a mate.

The female of one firefly species has a trick. She copies the light codes of other species. When males from other species fly toward her to mate, she eats them instead!

Insect Clean-Up Crew

The world is a more pleasant place because of dung beetles. There are more than 30,000 species of these beetles. They clean up manure dropped by large mammals.

Some beetles shape the dung into round lumps the size of baseballs. A dung ball might be three times the size of the beetle itself.

A dung beetle rolls a ball of dung to its nest.

Nevertheless, these amazing beetles can roll the dung balls home to their nests.

Rolling dung is too much work for some beetles. Instead, they dig their nests under fresh piles of manure. Male and female beetles work together to fill underground rooms with the dung. These adults eat the dung. It also makes great baby food when their eggs hatch!

The early settlers of Australia brought cattle with them. Soon, the manure piled up, and the grass began to die. There were no dung beetles in Australia. The solution was to bring in dung beetles from Africa. In a few years, the beetles cleared away the dung, and the grass was green again.

The Helpful Ladybug

Beetles cause billions of dollars of crop damage every year. Boll weevils destroy cotton crops. Nut weevils bore into nuts. Japanese beetles attack grain crops. Colorado beetles go after potatoes. Wood-boring beetles weaken farm buildings. For farmers, beetles can be serious pests!

Each year, boll weevils cause great damage by destroying cotton crops.

Luckily, though, one beetle is a farmer's friend. This is the ladybug. The two-spotted ladybug is the most common in the United States. Its bright red "back" is actually a pair of wing covers. These wing covers hide the top of the insect's body.

Although it is small, the ladybug is a killer. It eats aphids and other insect pests. By doing this, it saves many important food and flower plants. Both adult ladybugs and those in the larva stage feed on small insects. The larvae, in particular, seem never to stop eating. Today, farmers buy ladybugs by the case and set them free in fields.

You may have heard the old nursery rhyme, "Ladybug, Ladybug, Fly Away Home!" Actually, though, farmers want ladybugs to stay in their fields. That way, the ladybugs will continue to eat insect pests. Scientists have recently bred a new ladybug. It looks the same, except that it has no wings. So it never flies away.

Ladybugs help farmers by eating insect pests.

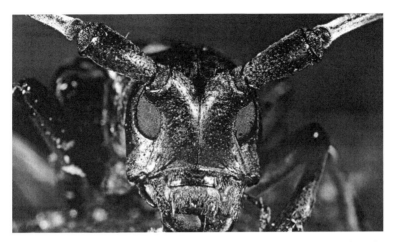
Asian long-horned beetles can destroy all trees in a neighborhood.

Beetle Invaders

In the mid-1990s, a deadly enemy attacked the United States. It was the Asian long-horned beetle. This black-and-white beetle suddenly appeared and began to do its damage. It is about 2 inches long. Though the beetle is harmless to people, it is deadly to trees.

The larvae of the long-horned beetle grow under the bark of trees. As they grow, they take all of the tree's food. Soon, they starve the tree to death. After destroying one tree, the adult beetles fly on to the next one. In a short while, they destroy all the trees in a neighborhood.

Scientists believe that the beetle probably arrived in the United States from China. The larvae may have been inside wooden packing cases. By 1996, trees in New York were dying. A few years later, the pest appeared in Chicago.

Destroying infested trees is the only way to get rid of this insect pest. When long-horned beetles appear, crews of workers move in. They have already taken down all the trees in some neighborhoods. Scientists are working hard to find a way to stop this insect pest.

Chapter Ten
Two Familiar Flies

There are about 120,000 different kinds of flies. The scientific name for flies is *Diptera*. This name means "two winged." Most insects have four wings, but flies have only two. Instead of a second pair of wings, flies have two small knobs on their backs. These knobs keep them balanced while they fly.

All flies eat liquid food. Some mop up juices from flowers or fruit. Some settle on the rotting remains of animals. Others bite live animals and feed on their blood. Two of the most common insect pests are flies. These pests are the mosquito and the housefly.

Flies have only two wings.

Bees have four wings.

The Life of the Mosquito

Mosquitoes are one of the flies that like blood. When a mosquito lands on you, it first cuts your skin with the jagged edges of its mouth. Then it puts a thin tube into the cut, and injects a watery liquid through this tube. This liquid makes the blood thin. Once the blood is thin enough, the mosquito sucks it up.

Only female mosquitoes bite. They need the blood to help their eggs grow. A female mosquito may carry up to 400 eggs in her body.

After she gets enough blood, the female mosquito lays her eggs in water. She tries to find water that has been standing awhile. Standing water usually contains tiny plants and animals. The mosquito larvae eat this food when they hatch. Ponds and puddles are good places for mosquitoes to breed. Ditches and old rubber tires filled with rainwater are good breeding places, too.

Mosquitoes breed in places where standing water collects.

The eggs hatch in a few days. Life is not easy for mosquito larvae. Fish and frogs attack them from below. Birds and other insects feed on them from above. After two weeks, the larvae that have survived grow into pupae.

Mosquito pupae move constantly. They rise to the surface of the water to breathe. They squirm away from danger. They move so much that they are called "tumblers."

53

After two or three days, the case around the tumbler splits open. Male mosquitoes appear first. A day later, the females come out. The adult mosquitoes need a few minutes to dry and spread their wings. Then they fly off, flapping their wings about 300 times per second.

Only female mosquitoes make a buzzing sound when they fly. The male uses his antennae to "hear" the female's buzzing. After mating, the male and female mosquito feed on plant nectar for about a week. Then the male dies. Alone, the female starts her search for blood.

Mosquito bites are annoying. They can also be dangerous. Some mosquitoes spread serious diseases such as malaria and yellow fever. Many cities control mosquitoes by spraying chemicals. A better solution is to drain the water where they breed.

The Life of a Housefly

The housefly is one of the most familiar insects on Earth. Houseflies do not bite. They are pests because they can carry serious diseases.

Outside, houseflies land on dead animals and garbage. Hairs on the fly's legs and body easily pick up germs from these animals and materials. Later, inside a house, a fly drops these germs onto food or kitchen surfaces.

Flies also spread disease when they eat. Because they cannot chew, everything a fly eats must be liquid. If a fly lands on your sandwich, for example, the first thing it will do is put saliva on it. The saliva is so strong that it turns solids into liquids. The fly will actually drink a tiny bit of your sandwich!

A little fly saliva is left behind when the fly leaves. Often, that saliva contains some of the fly's last meal. Its last meal may have been a dead mouse or dog manure.

In this way, flies spread deadly diseases such as cholera, polio, and typhoid.

The housefly is a good example of how fast insects multiply. If all the offspring of a single pair of houseflies lived for six months, they would produce about 190,000,000,000,000,000,000 flies. That would be enough to pile 47 feet of flies over the entire Earth! However, most fly eggs do not survive. They are eaten by other animals or killed by bad weather or disease.

A female fly lays more than 100 eggs at a time. During her short life, she may lay up to 20 batches of eggs. Usually, flies lay their eggs in animal manure, dead animals, or rotting plants. The eggs hatch in less than a day.

Fly larvae are often called **maggots**. Maggots grow quickly. In a week, they are 800 times heavier than they were when they hatched. (If humans grew this fast, a week-old baby would weigh 3 tons!) Soon, the maggots turn into pupae, their resting stage.

During the pupa stage, the old body parts of a maggot turn into liquid. Then this liquid turns into jelly. Finally, the jelly hardens into an adult fly. This change takes less than a week.

An adult housefly can live as long as two months. That is a long time for a fly. Some types of flies live only a few hours. A housefly's long life gives it plenty of time to lay many eggs.

Houseflies are much less of a problem today than they were in the past. We can thank Henry Ford for this great change. Ford made some of the first automobiles. He made cars cheaply, so more people could buy them.

Before cars took over the roads, people traveled on horseback or in horse-drawn wagons. These horses left piles of manure along the streets. That manure was a great breeding ground for flies. Once horses left the streets, the number of houseflies dropped quickly.

Chapter Eleven
Friend or Enemy?

No one likes to find an ant in a sugar bowl, a moth hole in a sweater, or termites in a basement. No one likes to be bitten by a mosquito or a horsefly. When an insect bites us, eats our food, or destroys our property, we call it a pest.

Less than 1 percent of all insects are pests. In the United States, just a few hundred insect species do all the damage. Still, the damage is expensive. The yearly bill for controlling insect pests and repairing their damage is more than $10 billion.

It is necessary to control harmful insects. Still, it is important to remember that insects do many good things. Bees carry pollen from flower to flower. Pollination helps plants to bear fruit. In this way, bees help make crops that are worth billions of dollars. Bees also provide millions of dollars worth of honey and wax every year. Silkworms give us silk. People enjoy the clothing made out of this beautiful cloth.

Bees pollinate flowers and other plants.

Insects are also part of nature's food chain. Birds, fish, and other animals depend on insects for food. Humans, in turn, eat these larger animals.

In many countries, people also eat insects. Chocolate-covered ants, fried caterpillars, and roasted termites are full of protein. In years to come, insects will probably provide a hungry world with more and more of its protein.

Insects also help break down dead animals and plants. That makes our world a cleaner, safer place. That also makes the soil richer. Insects that live in the ground also enrich the soil. Richer soil, in turn, helps plants to grow.

Insects are also helpful when they prey on other insects. As you have read, ladybugs eat many insects that destroy crops. Many wasps feed on caterpillars that destroy garden plants. In a way, insects themselves are the safest and easiest form of pest control.

Finally, even insects that feed on living animals and plants have a helpful side. In the long run, these "pests" are a necessary part of the great web of life. They help keep the total number of plants and animals on Earth in balance. As a result, our world is a richer and more interesting place.

Amazing Insect Facts

■ Army ants have no eyes. They find their victims by smell. Millions of them form a column a few feet wide. Then they smell out anything that is dead or alive.

■ A termite queen can lay an egg every two seconds, night and day. Some queens live for several years and lay more than a million eggs. Some queens are so filled with eggs that they are 160 times bigger than their male mates!

A termite queen lays more than a million eggs in its lifetime.

■ Tear moths from Southeast Asia feed on the tears of large animals. Settling close to the eye, the moth drinks the tear with its long feeding tube.

■ When seeking a horse, cow, or deer to bite, the female horsefly can cover many miles. Once she spots her target, she lands on its neck or some other hard-to-reach spot.

■ Painted lady butterflies are champion fliers. Some set out from North Africa and migrate across the Arctic Circle in Scandinavia. That's a distance of 1,800 miles (2,900 km)!

■ Cicadas are slow developers. One species takes 17 years to mature underground. Another takes 12 years. Responding to a mysterious signal, millions of them emerge all at once. They mate, lay eggs, and die—and then the long cycle begins again.

Every 12 or 17 years, cicadas hatch by the millions.

■ The darkling beetle lives in the super-dry Namib Desert in Africa. The only water there is mist rolling in from the sea. So the beetle points its abdomen into the wind and lets the water condense on its body.

■ A flea can jump 100 times its own height. A human jumping 100 times his or her own height could leap over 40-story buildings!

■ Many small insects, such as aphids and thrips, are too light to make much headway when they fly. So they let the wind do the work, blowing them from one place to another.

■ The male mole cricket has one of the loudest calls in the insect world. The cricket rubs its front wings together to make the call. The cricket's Y-shaped underground home then makes the sound louder, like a megaphone. Often, the call can be heard for more than $\frac{1}{2}$ mile.

■ The water beetles called whirligigs can see above and below the water at the same time. Half of each eye looks up, and half of each eye looks down.

■ Some African termites build houses out of dirt above the ground. Some of these houses are 20 feet high and 12 feet thick.

Some African termites build giant dirt houses above the ground.

■ The walking stick insect looks just like a twig. Sitting on a branch, the insect looks like part of the tree. In spring, the walking stick is green, like the new leaves. As it grows older, it turns brown, the color of the branches where it lives.

■ Many people think cockroaches are the world's most frightening bugs. One of the reasons is that they bleed white blood. A cockroach can also live for about a week after its head has been cut off!

■ A wood-boring beetle holds the record for the longest life cycle. It can spend 51 years inside the same piece of lumber!

GLOSSARY

abdomen (AB də mən)
the last of the three main body parts of an insect. It contains the digestive and reproductive organs. (10)

antenna (an TEN ə) (*plural* **antennae**)
sometimes called a feeler; insects use the antennae on their heads to smell and touch. (9)

blood vessel (blud VES əl)
a tube in the body that carries blood (17)

camouflage (CAM ə flahzh)
the colors, shapes, or structures that help an animal blend in with its surroundings (23)

chrysalis (KRIS ə lis)
the hard case in which a butterfly rests during its pupa stage (40)

circulatory system (SER cyə lə TOR ee SIS təm)
the parts of the body that work together to carry blood through the body (16)

complete metamorphosis (kəm PLEET met ə MOR fə sis)
a process of insect growth and change that occurs in four stages: egg, larva, pupa, adult (14)

compound eye (KAHM pownd eye)
an eye with many lenses (8)

crop (krahp)
a part of an insect's digestive system that stores partly digested food and breaks it down further (18)

digest (də JEST)
break down food so the body can use it (17)

digestive system (də JES tiv SIS təm)
the parts of the body that work together to break down food (17)

evaporate (i VAP ə RAYT)
change from a liquid to a vapor, or gas (37)

exoskeleton (EK soh SKEL ə tən)
the strong, light, outer skeleton of insects (8)

fungus (FUNG gəs)
a type of small plant that has no leaves and multiplies by spores; includes mushrooms and molds (30)

ganglion (GANG glee ən) (*plural* **ganglia**)
a tight cluster of nerve cells that controls walking, flying, and breathing (18)

grub (GRUB)
larva of a beetle (46)

honeydew (HUN ee DOO)
sweet, sticky liquid from plants (30)

hover (HUV ər)
   hang or fly in one place (10)
larva (LAR və) (*plural* **larvae**)
   the creature that hatches from the egg of an insect and undergoes complete metamorphosis (14)
lens (lenz)
   the part of the eye that focuses light (8)
maggot (MAG ət)
   the wormlike larva of a fly (55)
metamorphosis (met ə MOR fə sis)
   the growth and change of insects from eggs to adulthood (13)
migrate (MEYE grayt)
   to travel from one place to another as the seasons change (41)
mimic (MIM ik)
   something that pretends to be something other than what it is (25)
nectar (NEK tər)
   a sweet fluid found in flowers (33)
nerve cords (nerv kordz)
   the threads that carry messages from an insect's brain to the rest of its body (18)
nervous system (NER vəs SIS təm)
   the parts of the body that work together to carry messages from the brain to the rest of the body (18)
order (OR dər)
   a group of related plants or animals (11)
pollination (PAHL ə NAY shən)
   the process of spreading flower dust, or pollen, from flower to flower (32)
pupa (PYOO pə) (*plural* **pupae**)
   the resting stage in the life of many insects; it occurs after the larva stage and before adulthood (14)
simple eye (SIM pəl EYE)
   an eye that has only one lens (8)
species (SPEE sheez)
   a group of related animals that are alike enough to mate with each other (5)
spiracles (SPIR ə kəlz)
   the holes on the abdomen of an insect, through which it breathes (10)
thorax (THOR aks)
   the middle part of an insect's body; it holds the legs and the wings (9)
tracheae (TRAY kee ee)
   the air tubes found throughout an insect's body (16)

INDEX

abdomen, 10
antennae, 9, 19–20
ants, 27–31
  Amazon ants, 28–29
  ant farmers, 30–31
  army ants, 29–30, 58
  honey ants, 31
  wood ants, 25
aphid(s), 5, 30–31, 50, 59

bees, 32–37
  drones, 33
  honeybees, 32, 35, 37
  queen, 33–34
  workers, 33–37
beetles, 46–51
  African ground beetle, 25
  boll weevils, 49
  bombardier beetle, 24
  Colorado beetles, 49
  darkling beetle, 59
  dung beetle, 47–49
  fireflies, 47–48
  fungus beetle, 46
  Goliath beetle, 6–7, 46
  Japanese beetles, 49
  ladybug, 47, 49–50
  long-horned beetle, 47, 51
  nut weevils, 49
  water beetles, 60
  wood-boring beetle, 49, 60
blood, 16–17
blood vessels, 17
butterflies, 38–42
  black swallowtail, 39–40
  caterpillar, 23–24, 40
  dwarf blue butterfly, 6
  Kallima butterfly, 24
  monarch, 24, 41–42
  painted lady butterflies, 58
  puss-moth caterpillar, 24
  viceroy, 42

camouflage, 23–24
chrysalis, 40
cicadas, 26, 59

circulatory system, 16
cockroaches, 22, 60
complete metamorphosis, 14–15
compound eyes, 8
cricket, 59
crop, 18

defenses of insects, 21–26
  camouflage, 23
  false horns, producing, 24
  flying/running away, 21–22
  mimicking, 25
  no-defense defense, 26
  numbers, strength in, 21
  playing dead, 23
  setting off bombs, 24
  smell, producing a terrible, 24
  squirting acid, 24
  stinging, 24
  tasting bad, 24
digest, 17
digestive system, 17
dragonflies, 5, 10, 12, 21

evaporates, 37
exoskeleton, 8

flea, 59
flies, 52–55
  horsefly, 58
  houseflies, 54–55
  maggots, 55
  mosquitoes, 52–54
  robber fly, 6
food chain, 46, 57
fossils, 5
fungus, 30

ganglia, 18
grasshoppers, 11–12, 14, 22
grubs, 46

honeydew, 30–31
horseflies, 18, 22, 58
hover, 10

Insecta, 11

lacewings, 21, 24
larva(e), 14, 50–51, 53, 55
lenses, 8
locusts, 5

metamorphosis, 13–15
migrating, 41
mimic, 25
moths, 43–45
  Atlas moth, 6
  Io, 44
  Luna, 44
  Polyphemus, 44
  silkworm, 43, 56
  tear moths, 58

nectar, 33
nerve cords, 18
nervous system, 18

orders, 11

parts of an insect, 8–11, 16, 19–20
  abdomen, 8, 10
  antennae, 9, 19–20
  head, 8–9
  legs, 9, 11
  mouths, 9
  spiracles, 10, 16
  thorax, 8–9
  tracheae, 16
  wings, 9–10
pest control, 56–57
pollination, 32, 56
pupa(e), 14, 40, 53, 55

senses, 18–20
simple eyes, 8
species, 5
spiracles, 10, 16
stinkbugs, 24

termite queen, 58
thorax, 8–9
thrips, 59
tracheae, 16

walking stick, 6, 60
wasps, 6, 11, 12, 57

Photo Credits